Lyme
Disease

Lyme
Disease

**Dr. Alvin Silverstein, Virginia Silverstein,
and Laura Silverstein Nunn**

Watts LIBRARY

Franklin Watts
A Division of Grolier Publishing
New York • London • Hong Kong • Sydney
Danbury, Connecticut

Note to readers: Definitions for words in **bold** can be found in the Glossary at the back of this book.

Photographs ©: Medichrome/StockShop: 35 (David York); Monkmeyer Press: 8 (Yale); New England Stock Photo: 21 (Grace Davies), 6 (Hubbell); Photo Researchers: 25 (Ken Brate), 5 bottom, 13, 28 (Scott Camazine), 33 (Russell D. Curtis), 26 (Ken Eward/SS), 24 (Oliver Meckes), 34 (Oliver Meckes/Gelderblom), 10, 22 (Hank Morgan/SS), 14 (Larry Mulvehill), 20 (Leonard Rue, Jr.), 19 (David Schleser/Nature's Images), 44 (John Serrao); PhotoEdit: 42 (Robert Brenner), 37 (Gary A. Conner), 16 (Tony Freeman), 30 (Spencer Grant), 5 top, 38 (Dwayne Newton), 41 (D. Young-Wolff); Tony Stone Images: cover (Robert Brons/BPS), 2 (Tom Stock); Visuals Unlimited: 15 (Bill Banaszewski), 11 (R. Calentine), 45 (Joe McDonald), 43 (G & C Merker).

The photograph on the cover shows a magnified deer tick on a human arm. Ticks like this one can spread the bacteria that cause Lyme disease when they bite an animal. The photograph opposite the title page shows a hiker who is not taking the proper precautions against Lyme disease.

Visit Franklin Watts on the Internet at: http://publishing.grolier.com

Library of Congress Cataloging-in-Publication Data

Alvin Silverstein, Virginia Silverstein, and Laura Silverstein Nunn.
    Lyme disease / by Alvin Silverstein, Virginia Silverstein, and Laura Silverstein Nunn
        p. cm.— (Watts Library)
    Includes bibliographical references and index.
    Summary: Discusses the causes, symptoms, and treatment of Lyme disease, as well as ways to protect against it.
    ISBN 0-531-11751-0 (lib. bdg.)   0-531-16531-0 (pbk.)
    1. Lyme disease—Juvenile literature. [1. Lyme disease. 2. Diseases.] I. Silverstein, Virginia B. II. Nunn, Laura Silverstein. III. Title. IV. Series.
RC155.5.S568 2000
616.9'2—dc21
        99-42674
        CIP

Contents

Chapter One
An Outdoor Danger 7

Chapter Two
What Is Lyme Disease? 17

Chapter Three
A Tick and Its World 23

Chapter Four
Diagnosis and Treatment 31

Chapter Five
Preventing Lyme Disease 39

46 **Timeline of Lyme Disease**

48 **Glossary**

53 **To Find Out More**

58 **A Note on Sources**

60 **Index**

This tree-lined street is typical of the quiet countryside near Lyme, Connecticut.

An Outdoor Danger

Polly Murray was excited when she and her husband moved to the quiet, countryside town of Lyme, Connecticut, in the mid-1950s. Their picture-perfect home was near the Connecticut River and surrounded by woods.

Nobody knew then that there was a danger in that peaceful looking countryside—a danger that came to be known as Lyme disease. This is a tick-borne disease spread by ticks that carry germs in their guts. Ticks are tiny spiderlike

No Sick Ticks

Ticks don't get Lyme disease. The germs that cause the illness multiply in their bodies, but don't make them sick.

animals that live in wooded areas and overgrown fields and lawns. They feed on the blood of other animals.

When a disease-carrying tick sucks an animal's blood, disease germs can enter the victim's body and make the victim sick. In most cases, Lyme disease can be treated with medicine soon after **symptoms** appear. But if the disease is not **diagnosed** soon after it starts, the symptoms may become more severe and treatment may become more difficult.

For people who live in tick-infested areas, summer is a time to think about Lyme disease—but it doesn't have to ruin your summertime plans. Let's talk about what you can do to protect yourself from Lyme disease and the ticks that carry it—how to be safe and still have fun—and how Polly Murray helped scientists learn about Lyme disease.

Summer is a time for carefree outdoor fun

The Discovery of Lyme Disease

Polly Murray and her growing family enjoyed living in Lyme until she became ill in the spring of 1956. She had a fever. Her whole body ached. In the years that followed, she was plagued by a variety of ailments, including headaches, fatigue, rashes, fevers, and stiff and swollen joints. The doctors told Polly that her symptoms were nothing to worry about. In the mid-1970s, though, the rest of her family began to have similar symptoms.

In the summer of 1975, Polly's husband had to use crutches because the joints in his knees were stiff and swollen. He also developed a rash on his back. Their daughter and three sons suffered from headaches and badly swollen knees. Even the family pets were ill.

That summer, the doctors said that one of the Murray boys had **juvenile rheumatoid arthritis (JRA)**. JRA is not a very common disease. When Polly talked to neighbors, however, she found out that in Lyme and the nearby towns eighteen other people had JRA. Some people also suffered from headaches, rashes, and fevers. What was going on around Lyme?

Disease Detectives

In October 1975, Polly called the Connecticut State Health Department and complained about the health problems in the Lyme area. Other people called with similar complaints. The state health officials brought in Allen Steere, who had worked

Researchers from the Connecticut State Health Department are trapping ticks to be tested for Lyme disease.

at the national Centers for Disease Control and Prevention (CDC).

By May 1976, Steere and his colleagues had found thirty-nine children and twelve adults apparently suffering from a similar form of arthritis—in a population of just 12,000. Normally, JRA affects about 1 child out of every 100,000. There were other hints that this was not normal JRA. JRA is not usually found in groups. In this case, though, half of the children affected lived on only four roads! JRA also does not usually strike more than one child in the same family—but in Lyme, it did.

In the summer of 1976, Steere and his colleagues announced the discovery of a disease they named "Lyme arthritis." The name was later changed to *Lyme disease* because arthritis isn't the only symptom associated with the disease.

Tracing the Cause

What could be causing this mysterious illness? Steere noticed some interesting patterns. First, most of the patients with Lyme disease got sick during the summer months. Also, about 25 percent of them reported having a rash that looked like a bull's eye before their arthritis set in. The researchers thought the rash could be caused by the bite of an insect or a tick. Such creatures are most likely to live in heavily wooded areas, and they are most active during the summer months.

In the summer of 1977, Steere found nine patients who remembered being bitten by ticks, and one of them had saved the tiny pinhead-sized tick. Steere and his colleagues found that it was a northern **deer tick** of a kind called *Ixodes*. Studies revealed that the deer tick was twelve times more common on the Lyme side of the Connecticut River than on the other shore, where the disease did not seem to occur.

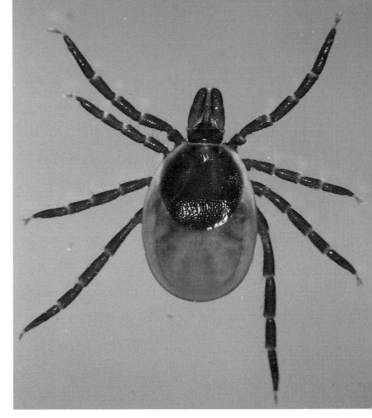

This is a female deer tick, Ixodes scapularis, *much bigger than life size.*

In 1979, the tick that spreads Lyme disease was identified as *Ixodes scapularis*. (ICKS-oh-dees skap-you-LAR-iss) This deer tick is found along the East Coast from Maine to Florida and in some parts of the north-central United States, such as Wisconsin and Minnesota.

Finding the Guilty Germ

Ticks do not cause Lyme disease, but they carry the germ that causes the symptoms. They spread this germ to other animals while they feed on the animals' blood. Although the

Who Are You?

Scientists originally thought that the tick that spreads Lyme disease was a new species. Later, they decided that the deer tick was actually a slightly different variety of *Ixodes scapularis*.

researchers had identified the disease carrier, they still didn't know what kind of germ was causing the disease. Tests for viruses were negative. There was some evidence that the germ was a **bacterium**, but none of the tests on Lyme patients had found which bacterium it was.

In 1913, a physician in Austria had speculated that ticks carry microscopic germs that could be passed on to the people that they bite. He suggested that researchers look for bacteria in the guts of ticks, but no one followed up on his suggestion. In the 1950s, some investigators thought they saw spiral-shaped bacteria in samples of skin from patients with the bull's-eye rash, but other researchers did not confirm their findings.

Then, in the fall of 1981, Willy Burgdorfer, an expert on tick-borne diseases, was studying a cluster of cases of Rocky Mountain spotted fever on Long Island, New York. Rocky Mountain spotted fever is a serious disease that is carried by a different kind of tick, and is caused by a tiny tick-borne parasite called a rickettsia. When Burgdorfer looked at deer ticks, which are plentiful on Long Island, he didn't find any rickettsias. He did find something interesting—tiny spiral-shaped bacteria called **spirochetes** (spy-ruh-KEETS) in the guts of the ticks. Burgdorfer then tested blood samples from Lyme disease patients to find out whether they had been exposed to these spirochetes. The tests were positive; the patients had been exposed to these bacteria.

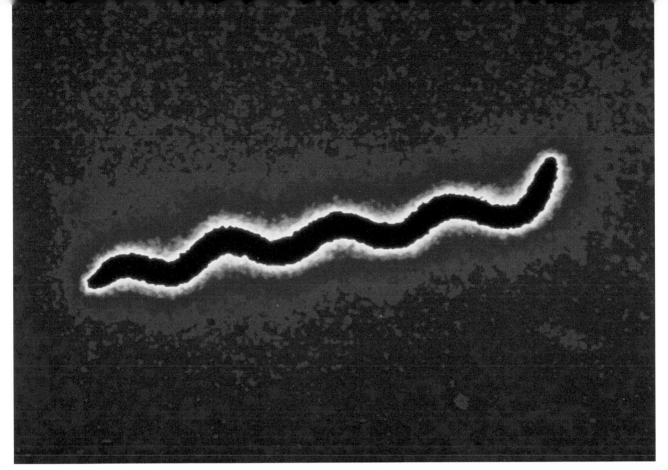

Soon afterward, Steere and his team grew the spirochetes from blood and skin samples from Lyme disease patients. These tests confirmed that the spirochetes, a new species of bacteria, were the cause of Lyme disease. In 1984, the germ was named *Borrelia burgdorferi* in honor of its discoverer.

This photograph shows a greatly magnified, color-enhanced view of Borrelia burgdorferi, the spirochete that causes Lyme disease.

A New Disease?

Lyme disease is not a new disease. It was first observed in Europe more than a century ago. In 1883 in Breslau, Germany, Alfred Buchwald described a skin disorder that was similar to the rash often seen in Lyme disease. In 1909, Arvid

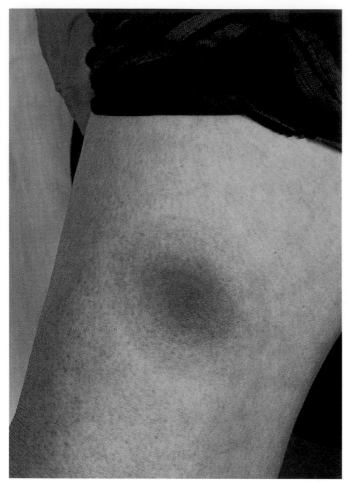

Erythema migrans is the name doctors use to describe the expanding red rash of Lyme disease

Afzelius, a Swedish doctor, reported an expanding ringlike red rash that developed in patients who were bitten by the sheep tick *Ixodes ricinus*. He called the rash **erythema migrans** (EM), meaning "migrating red rash." Doctors gradually found that a number of other medical problems can follow the EM rash, including **arthritis**, nerve problems, heart problems, and **meningitis**.

In Europe in 1955, several doctors injected themselves with bits of skin from a patient with EM. They all developed a similar rash, which they were able to cure with penicillin, an **antibiotic**. This showed that EM was caused by a germ.

Old-time Specimens

In 1995, when ticks taken from a Hungarian cat and an Austrian fox in the 1880s were analyzed, scientists found *B. burgdorferi*. Then tests on **deoxyribonucleic acid (DNA)** taken from the skin of white-footed mice and chipmunks, collected in 1894 by a researcher at a Massachusetts museum, showed that they also contained *B. burgdorferi*. These tests proved that Lyme disease has actually been in Europe and the United States for more than 100 years.

Why Is It Spreading Now?

If Lyme disease has been around for more than a century, why have so many more cases been found in the last 25 years? The answer seems to lie in a change in the environment. During the 1800s, settlers cut down forests to make room for pastures and farms. As a result, white-tailed deer, which carry ticks and like to live on the edge of forests, almost became extinct. Without deer, ticks could not thrive.

Then in the 1900s, farming became less profitable and many farmers shut down their farms. As a result, the forests eventually grew back—and so did the deer population. Meanwhile, people from the cities moved out to "the country." More houses in wooded areas gave deer ticks more chances to bite humans.

White-tailed deer thrive in wooded areas near rural and suburban homes, providing opportunities for Lyme disease bacteria to spread to humans.

Outdoor hobbies, such as hiking, may expose people to ticks carrying Lyme disease.

Chapter Two

What Is Lyme Disease?

Anybody can get Lyme disease. Children are more likely than adults to get it because young people often spend more time exploring and playing outside. Adults who spend time outdoors, such as landscapers and loggers, or people with outdoor hobbies, such as hunting or fishing, also have a higher risk of getting Lyme disease. Even pets can get Lyme disease if they spend time outside, and they can bring disease-carrying ticks into the home too.

Tick Country

Ticks live mainly in wooded areas and tall grasses. A tick may attach itself to your body while you're walking in the woods or having a picnic in a country field, but you can also be bitten right in your own backyard. Ticks are not usually found in open lawns with short grass because they dry out very quickly in the open. They thrive where the humidity is high—in the leaf litter on the forest floor, for example, or in low-growing shrubs and plants at the edge of a wooded area. Lyme disease is not a big problem in cities, but it is a growing danger in suburbs and housing developments that are close to woods and fields.

Most cases of Lyme disease have been reported in parts of New York, New Jersey, Connecticut, Rhode Island, Massachusetts, Pennsylvania, Minnesota, Wisconsin, and California, but Lyme disease can occur almost anywhere in the United States. Cases of Lyme disease have also been reported in Asia and Europe.

What Causes Lyme Disease?

You cannot catch Lyme disease by touching an infected person or animal. You can get Lyme disease only if you are bitten by a tick that is carrying the tiny, spiral-shaped bacterium *B. burgdorferi*. Not all deer ticks carry the bacteria. In areas where there is little or no Lyme disease, only 1 percent of deer ticks are infected with *B. burgdorferi*. In areas where Lyme disease is

Who's to Blame?

People are quick to blame deer for the spread of Lyme disease, but white-footed mice are more likely than deer to spread it. Ticks are not born with the Lyme disease spirochete. They become infected when they suck blood from animals that are infected with the germ. One infected mouse can pass the bacteria to hundreds of young deer ticks. The ticks then spread the germ to other animals. Unlike mice (and people), deer do not become infected by *B. burgdorferi*. They merely provide food for the ticks.

endemic—where there are a lot of cases—more than 50 percent of the deer ticks may carry the bacteria.

Spotting the Symptoms

For many people, the first sign of Lyme disease is an expanding red rash. As it grows, the center may clear up and look like normal skin again. The rash can get very large and spread rapidly. This is EM, the migrating rash that was first described in Europe a century ago. Approximately one-third of EM rashes look like a series of red and pink rings—a bull's eye.

About 90 percent of people with Lyme disease have an EM rash, even though one-third do not recall a tick bite. EM develops at the site of the tick bite and can be seen as early as 1 or 2 days after the bite, or as late as a month afterward. Some people have many rashes on different parts of the body, but this does not mean that they had many tick bites. Spirochetes that entered through one bite can move into a person's bloodstream and spread to other parts of the body.

Days, even weeks, after the tick bite, other symptoms may appear. They often resemble the symptoms of other illnesses, which makes diagnosis of Lyme disease difficult. Some common symptoms include fever, sore throat, and a feeling of tiredness. Other viruslike symptoms are very uncommon in Lyme disease. If you have a runny nose or diarrhea, you probably have a viral infection. Lyme disease symptoms are often unpredictable—they may come and go. They may even occur in different parts of the body.

Did You Know?

Some people develop a small red rash around a tick bite even though they do not have Lyme disease. This rash is caused by irritation from the bite and soon goes away by itself.

Lyme Disease and Your Pets

Dogs and cats have a high risk of getting Lyme disease. People used to believe that cats don't get Lyme disease, but now we know that they do. Dogs seem to get Lyme disease more often. It is possible that a cat's frequent grooming removes ticks that have not latched on to the animal yet.

More serious complications may develop if Lyme disease is not identified until months after the tick bite. If it is left untreated, Lyme disease can cause problems with the heart or nervous system. People with heart problems may feel dizzy, have an irregular heartbeat, and have trouble breathing. Problems with the nervous system may cause headaches, stiff neck, and difficulty concentrating and remembering. Another late feature of *B. burgdorferi* infection is arthritis, most often affecting the knees. All these symptoms might sound alarming, but not all tick bites lead to Lyme disease—and all the problems caused by Lyme disease are treatable.

These black-legged ticks (Ixodes scapularis) were collected in Connecticut. They will be examined for Lyme disease.

Chapter Three

A Tick and Its World

Hundreds of kinds of ticks are found in North America, but only a few carry the bacterium that causes Lyme disease. Most Lyme disease cases are caused by the **black-legged tick**, commonly known as the deer tick (*Ixodes scapularis*). The deer tick is found in the northeastern and midwestern states. The tick that spreads Lyme disease along the Pacific Coast is the **western black-legged tick** (*Ixodes pacificus*). There is some evidence that the **lone star tick** (*Amblyomma* *americanum*), found in the southern and southeastern states, can also spread Lyme disease.

Portrait of a Tick

Many people think of all small, crawly creatures, including ticks, as insects. Ticks are not insects, though. Both ticks and spiders belong to a group of animals called **arachnids**, which comes from a Greek word meaning "spider." Like spiders, ticks have eight legs, while insects have six legs.

A magnified view of an Ixodes *tick on a leaf.*

Ticks are **parasites**. They live by feeding on other animals—their **hosts**. Instead of killing their prey, ticks hitch a ride on a suitable host and feed by sucking their host's blood. Many kinds of animals can serve as hosts—dogs, cats, birds, deer, mice, horses, cattle, and people.

An Acorn Connection?

A mature oak tree usually produces about 1,000 acorns in a year. Every 3 or 4 years, however, as many as 50,000 acorns drop to the ground. A huge acorn crop can lead to a population explosion among white-footed mice, which feed on acorns. The mouse population may reach twenty times its normal level, providing a plentiful food supply for young deer ticks, which soon have their own population explosion. That means more Lyme disease.

A Tick Up Close

Under a magnifying glass, you can see that a tick has a large, rather flattened body and a very small head. A microscope reveals more details:

- The tick's legs have many joints. The tip of each leg has sticky pads that help the tick cling to its host, and each leg ends in a claw.

- Each tick has two **palps** or feelers that serve as sense organs. They are covered with hairs and other sensitive structures that help the tick find a host.
- Between the two palps is a very specialized mouth called the **hypostome**. It is long, slim, and covered with barbs, like the barbs on a fishhook. The tick uses its mouth to drill a hole in the host's skin. When the tip of the hypostome enters a tiny blood vessel, the barbs hold the tick in place while it sucks up blood.

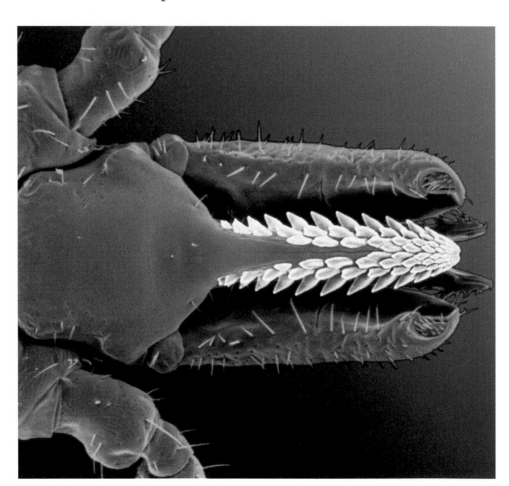

This photograph shows a close-up view of a tick's mouthparts, including its two palps (feelers) and the barbed hypostome, which drills into its victim's skin.

- A tick produces a chemical called cementum that helps its mouthparts stick more firmly to it's victim's skin. It is so strong that a bit of the tick's mouthparts may stay attached to the skin even after you have done your best to remove the tick.

A tick usually takes a rather long time to attach itself to a host. Typically, it climbs aboard near someone's ankle and then starts crawling upward, seeking a warm, moist place where it can settle down to feed. Most bites are found behind the knees, near the groin, at the beltline, or in the armpits. More than 24 hours may pass from the time a tick first hitches a ride until it starts to feed. It may be another 24 to 36 hours after the time the tick begins to feed before *B. burgdorferi* enters the host's body.

A Tick's Life

Ticks live only 2 years. A tick begins life as a tiny **egg** and passes through a series of developmental stages on its way to adulthood. At each stage, it looks somewhat different from its former self, and it behaves differently too.

A tick's **life cycle** has four stages: egg, larva, nymph, and adult. An adult female tick lays her eggs in the spring. About a month later, tiny larvae hatch out of the eggs. A **larva** has six legs, rather than the eight it will have as an adult tick. The larva gets its first feeding from a small animal, most likely a mouse, and may pick up *B. burgdorferi*. This feeding lasts

Three deer ticks on a finger: the smallest is a nymph, the middle-sized tick is an adult male, and the largest is an adult female.

Nasty Nymphs

Deer ticks can spread Lyme disease as nymphs or adults. But the nymphs are more likely to spread the disease because they are most active during the summer months, when many people are outdoors. Nymphs are also harder to spot than adult ticks.

about 2 days until the larva becomes **engorged,** or swollen with blood. The larva then drops off and hides in a safe, cozy place until the following spring. During this time, its body goes through some changes.

In the spring the larvae **molt**—they shed their outer covering and emerge as eight-legged **nymphs**. Nymphs, or young ticks, are most active between June and August, but you may see them as early as May. During these months, they search for a second feeding, most likely from a white-footed mouse, but they can feed on other small animals and people too. This period, when the nymphs are searching for a meal, is known as the "Lyme disease season." The summertime feeding usually lasts 2 to 4 days. When the nymph becomes engorged, it drops off and crawls away to rest in a quiet place.

At the end of the summer, the nymph molts and changes into a fully developed **adult tick.** This is the final stage of its life cycle; it will not change anymore. An adult tick attaches itself to any available host. It needs a third feeding to form the sex cells that will produce a new generation of ticks. The adult male only needs to make enough sperm—male sex cells—for mating. It feeds only briefly, mates, and dies soon afterward. The female must eat much more so that she can provide a food supply for her eggs. She lives through the winter and in the spring lays as many as 2,500 eggs!

The deer tick is very small—even for a tick. The immature nymphs that spread Lyme disease are about the size of a poppy seed. When ticks are feeding, their bodies may become three times their original size. Normally, deer tick nymphs are brownish-black, but they turn grayish when they are engorged with blood.

> ## A Big Difference
>
> The **American dog tick,** *Dermacentor variabilis*, also called a wood tick, is often mistaken for the deer tick. There is a big difference in size though. The dog tick is much larger. It is about the size of a watermelon seed. The dog tick's color and markings are different too. The dog tick does not carry Lyme disease, but it can carry other diseases, such as Rocky Mountain spotted fever.

An adult deer tick is about the size of a sesame seed. The adult female is brick-red, with a black shield on her back. (After feeding, the female turns blue-black and may swell up to the size of a pea.) The adult male is all black and somewhat smaller than the female. It's easy to miss seeing a tiny tick on your body—so look carefully.

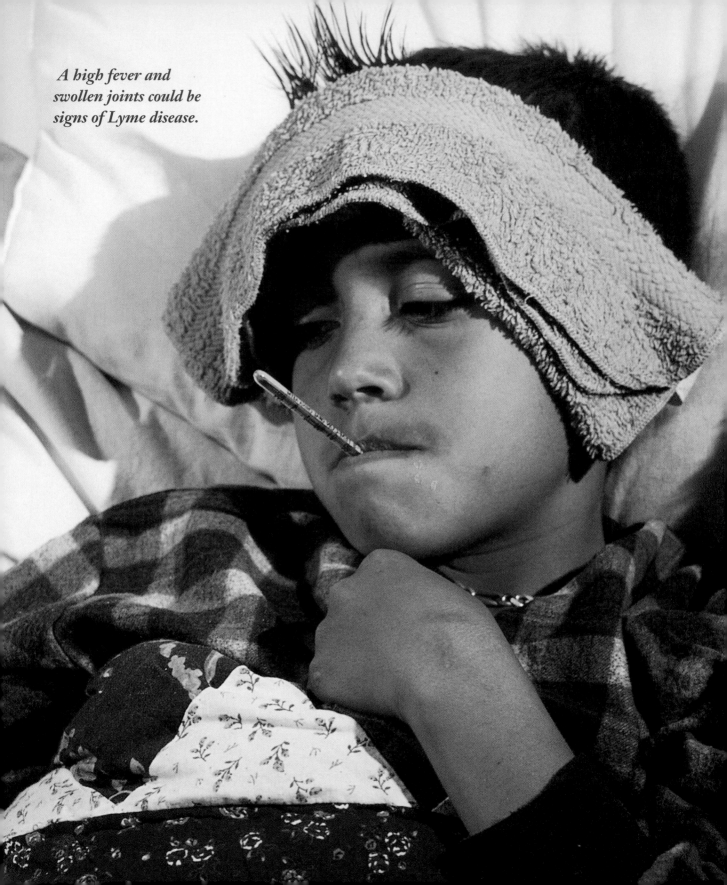

A high fever and swollen joints could be signs of Lyme disease.

Chapter Four

Diagnosis and Treatment

One May afternoon, 8-year-old Cory came down with a high fever. The next day, the fever was gone and Cory seemed fine. About a week later, however, Cory started to walk with a limp. His ankle was swollen, and it hurt when anything touched his foot.

The doctor ordered an X ray of Cory's leg but found no broken bones. However, the family lived in a tick-infested area, and it was possible that Cory had Lyme disease. The doctor took a blood sample to run some tests, but the results would not be ready for several days. In the meantime, a pediatric specialist examined Cory's leg and was certain that the swollen ankle was arthritis caused by Lyme disease. After talking with the specialist, Cory's family doctor started him on antibiotics. By the time the blood test came back positive—showing that Cory had Lyme disease—he was already feeling better.

Doctors are becoming more familiar with Lyme disease. Patients are less likely to go undiagnosed and untreated than they were in the early days of the disease. In fact, some medical experts believe that a bigger problem is a tendency to diagnose Lyme disease in patients who do not really have the illness.

How to Know

In diagnosing Lyme disease, a doctor usually starts by collecting information. The doctor may ask many questions, including:

- Where do you live?
- Do you spend any time outside?
- Have you been bitten by a tick?
- What are your symptoms?
- Does anyone else in your family have any health problems?

The most obvious pieces of evidence for Lyme disease are a tick bite and the bull's-eye rash. But not everybody gets the typical skin rash, and many people with Lyme disease don't remember getting bitten by a tick. A deer tick bite can easily go unnoticed. The other symptoms of Lyme disease are not always obvious, and other diseases can cause some of the same symptoms.

Laboratory tests are needed to determine whether a person has been infected by the Lyme disease spirochete. However, doctors often treat people on the basis of their symptoms and background information before the test results come back. They do this because the symptoms usually need immediate attention, and the tests may not show the presence of the infection during the early stages.

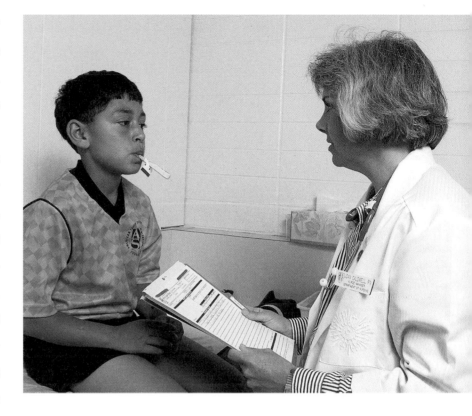

This doctor is evaluating a child for Lyme disease. She may begin treatment before test results come back.

Laboratory Tests

The tests used most often are the **ELISA test (enzyme-linked immunosorbent assay)** and the **Western blot test**. The ELISA test is cheaper and faster than the Western blot, but it is not as accurate. Doctors can use the Western blot as a follow-up test to confirm positive results from the ELISA test. Neither of these blood tests actually identifies the Lyme disease spirochete in the blood, however. Instead, the tests detect

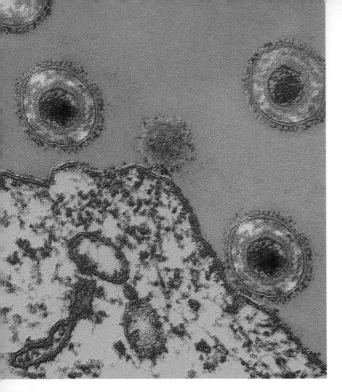

The three chickenpox viruses shown in this photo are about to attack a body cell. Some diseases, like chickenpox, are caused by viruses. Others, like Lyme disease, are caused by bacteria. No matter what causes a disease, though, the body makes antibodies to fight against it.

antibodies—special proteins that the body makes to attack foreign invaders such as viruses and bacteria.

When a person gets Lyme disease, the body makes antibodies specially designed to fight *B. burgdorferi*. After the battle is over, these antibodies stay in the body. In some illnesses, such as chickenpox or measles, antibodies protect the person from later attacks by the same kind of germs. The person becomes **immune** to that disease and will never get it again. The antibodies that stay in the body after Lyme disease do not protect the person from another attack by *B. burgdorferi* bacteria. You can get Lyme disease again and again.

Troublesome Tests

Lyme disease tests sometimes give false results. The tests look for antibodies, but the antibodies may not be detectable for more than 4 to 6 weeks after the tick bite. The tests may give a false negative result, indicating that there is no Lyme disease. On the other hand, the antibodies produced during other illnesses may be so similar to those of Lyme disease that they give a false positive result, indicating that the disease is present even if it is not. People who are being tested for a second bout with Lyme disease may not get accurate test results because they still have antibodies from the previous infection.

The **PCR test** is a different kind of Lyme disease test. The PCR test identifies the DNA of the Lyme disease spirochete itself, rather than the antibodies that the infected person produces against it. This test is not widely used because it is expensive and takes longer than antibody tests. Like the other tests, the PCR test can give false results if the blood or tissue sample does not contain enough bacteria, or if the sample was contaminated.

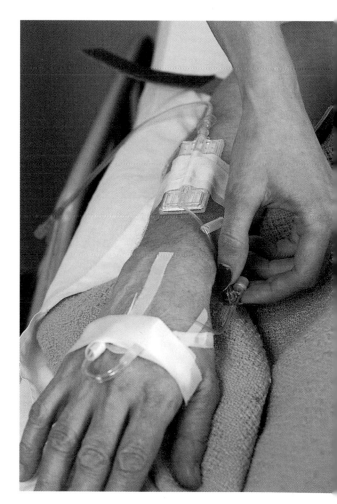

This patient is receiving IV treatment through a blood vessel in his hand.

Antibiotic Assault

Lyme disease can be successfully treated with antibiotics. The drugs commonly used to treat Lyme disease are the antibiotics amoxicillin and doxycycline, but treatment is not the same for everyone. The treatment depends on the severity of the disease and the patient's symptoms. Lyme disease is easiest to treat when it is caught early. Drugs given by mouth can destroy the Lyme disease bacteria quickly, and the symptoms usually disappear within a couple of weeks.

In the later stages of Lyme disease, treatment may be more complicated. Some symptoms may go away for a while, then reappear unex-pectedly. People with Lyme arthritis or problems with the heart or nervous system may need more intensive therapy.

Some people need **IV (intravenous) treatments.** A hollow needle is inserted into a person's vein, and the antibiotic, mixed with saltwater, is dripped directly into the person's blood through a tube. In serious cases of Lyme disease, the person may not be cured for months or even years after the treatment is begun.

Ready, Set, Go

It's not always easy for doctors to know when to start treatment for Lyme disease. When an EM rash is present, the diagnosis is clear, and doctors can start the treatment immediately—even before they receive test results. If someone has been bitten by a tick and did not get a rash or if there are no other obvious signs of the disease, the decision is a bit more difficult.

In such cases, most doctors choose not to start antibiotics before they get test results. Antibiotics can have bad side effects. Because some bacteria resist drugs, if antibiotics are used too often, these bacteria may multiply and spread. Doctors worry that drug-resistant germs may become so common that the antibiotics used to fight them may lose their effectivness.

In the Long Run

Medical experts say that Lyme disease patients should take antibiotics for 21 to 30 days. If the drug therapy is stopped before it has killed all the bacteria, the symptoms may come back. Some patients continue to have symptoms for several months or even years.

Some patients may have long-lasting symptoms because the infection caused severe damage. The body's repairs can sometimes take a long time. Some patients develop a "post-Lyme disease syndrome" that includes sleep disorders, fatigue, and aches. Some doctors believe that these problems may occur because bacteria hide out in the brain or other parts of the body and escape the drug treatment. Another possibility is that the patient may have been reinfected by another tick bite. Some patients with Lyme disease may develop an unrelated illness and think the symptoms of the new illness are due to Lyme disease.

Post-Lyme disease syndrome can cause sleep disorders as well as a variety of other symptoms.

To avoid picking up ticks, tuck the bottoms of your pants legs into your socks before going into the woods.

Chapter Five

Preventing Lyme Disease

Don't panic and think that you're automatically going to get Lyme disease if you set foot outdoors during the summer months. There are many simple and effective ways to protect yourself against tick bites and the diseases they can spread. There are new vaccines that may help protect people against the Lyme disease spirochete. Also, researchers have developed ways to reduce the tick population in the wild, which will hopefully reduce the number of Lyme disease cases. What can you do to protect yourself from ticks and Lyme disease? Here are some tips:

- Stay away from tick-infested areas, such as overgrown lawns and fields. Keep your lawn cut short. Ticks like moist areas, where they can't be dried out by the hot sun.
- If you go hiking, don't wander off the trails. Stay in the center of the path, away from bushes and long, overhanging blades of grass. On deer paths, ticks are often found on the shrubs at the edges of the path.
- Wear light-colored clothing so that ticks are easier to spot.
- Wear closed shoes and tuck the bottoms of your pants into your socks so ticks can't get to your skin.
- Spray **pesticides**—chemicals that kill animals such as insects or ticks—on your clothes, but not on your skin. Pesticides may cause skin irritation or other health problems.

The Art of Tick Removal

If you find a tick on your body, don't panic and rip it out. Squeezing the tick may cause its body fluids to leak out. Those fluids may then slip through breaks in your skin and infect you.

The best thing to do is to ask an adult to remove the tick. It should be taken out with tweezers or a commercial tick-removal tool. Grab the tick as close to its mouthparts as possible, trying to avoid the tick's swollen body. Then dab the tick bite with an antiseptic to prevent infection. Carefully throw the tick away so its bacteria don't spread.

- When you get home, wash your clothes to remove any hidden ticks.
- Take a shower to wash away any ticks that have not latched on yet.
- Have a parent check you very carefully for ticks. (Remember that a deer tick is so small it may look like a speck of dirt.)

Lyme Disease Vaccines

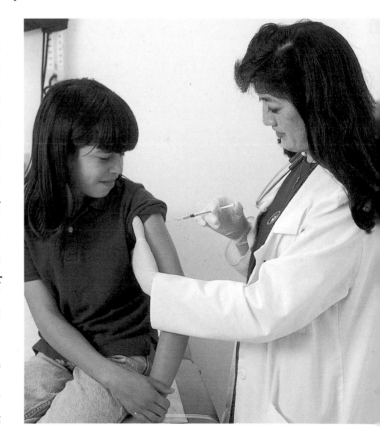

This girl is receiving a vaccine shot so she will be protected from Lyme disease.

Vaccines protect people against many diseases caused by bacteria and viruses. Before 1998, the only Lyme disease vaccine on the market was a vaccine for animals. Researchers worked hard to develop a Lyme disease vaccine safe enough to be used on people. In December 1998, the Food and Drug Administration (FDA) approved the first Lyme disease vaccine for people who live or work in tick-infested areas. This vaccine, containing a protein from the outer surface of *B. burgdorferi* called **OspA** (outer-surface protein A), may help thousands of people protect themselves against the disease.

Vaccines stimulate a person's body to produce antibodies, which set up a defense system to fight off specific disease germs. In fighting Lyme disease, however, the antibodies enter the disease-carrying tick and attack the bacteria inside the tick's body. The germ never has a chance to enter the person's body.

How does this happen? The vaccine causes the person to make antibodies against OspA, which covers the spirochete while it is inside the tick. As soon as the tick begins to feed on a vaccinated person, the anti-OspA antibodies in the host's blood are sucked into the tick's gut. When the antibodies attack the OspA protein in the tick, the bacterium's outer covering is destroyed and the spirochetes die.

People must take three doses of the vaccine over the course of a year to get full protection. After the first two shots of the vaccine, which are given a month apart, the vaccine is only 50 percent effective. After the third shot, which is given 1 year after the original vaccination, the vaccine is only about 80 percent effective.

Another vaccine, now under development, will include both OspA and another *B. burgdorferi* protein, **DbpA** (decorin-binding protein A). The spirochete uses this protein to attach to decorin, a protein found in human

People thinking about getting vaccinated against Lyme disease should talk about it with their doctor.

skin and connective tissue. Researchers hope that the "second-generation vaccine," containing two different *B. burgdorferi* proteins, will be even more effective against Lyme disease. Because neither vaccine provides any protection against other tick-borne diseases, however, people who get the Lyme disease vaccine should continue to protect themselves against tick bites.

Lucky Lizards

Lyme disease bacteria do not infect Western fence lizards. Researchers have found that the blood of these lizards contains a substance that kills *B. burgdorferi*, both in the lizards' bodies and in the ticks that feed on them. Scientists are trying to identify the bacteria-killing chemical in the lizards' blood. They hope it can be used in a vaccine or treatment for Lyme disease.

Breaking the Cycle

Researchers are also trying to find other ways to reduce the risk of Lyme disease by reducing the population of deer ticks. For example, they have set out tubes of pesticide-treated cotton balls for white-footed mice. The mice take the cotton balls home to line their nests, and the pesticide kills the ticks without hurting the mice. Unfortunately, this approach has not been effective in places where Lyme disease is most common, such as Westchester, New York, and rural New Jersey. It is possible that there are just too many mice in these areas.

Researchers are also looking at the deer tick's other favorite host—deer. Scientists have built special feeding stations where

Young white-footed mice in their nest

Guinea Hens on Guard

A few years ago, supermodel Christie Brinkley got Lyme disease at her estate on Long Island. Ticks were so plentiful on her land that she wore fishing boots to walk to the beach. Determined to fight Lyme disease, she bought some guinea hens, which are used in Africa to keep ticks out of barnyards. The guinea hens greatly reduced the tick population, but they are very noisy. So while guinea hens can help to cut the tick population, they may create problems with the neighbors.

deer are dusted with pesticide while they eat. These treatments help to cut down the number of adult deer ticks and thus reduce the next generation of Lyme disease-spreading pests.

Other studies are aimed at finding natural enemies of ticks, such as parasitic wasps that lay their eggs in the ticks' bodies. These efforts may someday help to make outdoor fun safer by reducing the risk of Lyme disease.

Timeline of Lyme Disease

1883	Alfred Buchwald of Breslau, Germany, described a serious skin disorder similar to the characteristic Lyme disease bull's-eye rash.
1884	*Ixodes* ticks attached to a cat in Hungary were collected, marked, and preserved. More than a century later, these specimens were found to be infected with *Borrelia burgdorferi*.
1888	*Ixodes* ticks attached to a fox in Austria were collected and stored. More than a century later, these specimens were found to be infected with *B. burgdorferi*.
1894	A researcher at a Massachusetts museum collected and preserved white-footed mice from Cape Cod. A century later, DNA testing showed that these mice were infected with Lyme disease bacteria.
1909	Swedish doctor Arvid Afzelius described the bull's-eye rash in patients who were bitten by the sheep tick, *Ixodes ricinus*. He called the rash erythema migrans (EM).
1913	Austrian physician B. Lipschütz speculated that ticks might carry germs in their guts.
1921	The first report of arthritis in patients following a tick bite is published.
1922	French doctors Charles Garin and Charles Bujadoux noticed a link between EM and nerve problems.
1934	German doctors noticed that some patients with EM rash and arthritis develop heart problems.

1949	Swedish doctor Sven Hellerström reported on cases of meningitis following EM.
1955	H. Gotz and colleagues injected themselves with skin from patients with the EM rash; they got the rash and cured it with penicillin.
1975	Polly Murray reported an outbreak of arthritis and other health problems in Lyme, Connecticut, and neighboring communities. Yale University researchers, led by Allen Steere and Stephen E. Malawista, started an investigation.
1979	Andrew Spielman of the Harvard School of Public Health identified the tick that causes Lyme disease as a new species, *Ixodes dammini*. It was later determined that the tick was not actually a distinct species.
1981	Willy Burgdorfer found spirochetes in ticks and linked them to Lyme disease.
1982	The Centers for Disease Control and Prevention started to keep track of Lyme disease cases.
1984	The Lyme disease bacterium was named *B. burgdorferi* in honor of Dr. Burgdorfer.
1993	Researchers determined that the deer tick that spreads Lyme disease belongs to the species *Ixodes scapularis*.
1998	The first Lyme disease vaccine, Lymerix, was approved. It is recommended for people who live or work in tick-infested areas.

Glossary

adult tick—a fully mature eight-legged tick in the final life-cycle stage. Adult ticks are most active during September to mid-October.

American dog tick—*Dermacentor variabilis*, also called the wood tick, is larger than the deer tick and is commonly found on pets

antibiotic—a medicine used to treat an illness caused by bacteria

antibody—a special protein that is produced in the body to attack foreign invaders such as viruses and bacteria

arachnid—an eight-legged invertebrate animal, such as a spider, scorpion, mite, or tick

arthritis—a condition in which the joints become swollen and painful

babesiosis—a tick-borne disease that can be spread by the deer tick, caused by the bacterium *Babesia microti*

bacterium (*plural* **bacteria**)—a germ; one-celled organism too small to see without a microscope. Some bacteria cause diseases when they get into the body.

black-legged tick—the deer tick

deer tick—black-legged tick (*Ixodes scapularis*), a tiny spider-like animal that is about the size of a poppy seed or sesame seed. It spreads Lyme disease in the eastern and midwestern United States and can also carry other disease bacteria.

deoxyribonucleic acid (DNA)—contains genetic material that determines an organism's characteristics

diagnosed—identified an illness

DbpA (decorin-binding protein A)— a protein of the Lyme disease spirochete that attaches to a protein (decorin) in human skin and connective tissue

egg—the first stage of a tick's life cycle

ehrlichiosis—a tick-borne disease that can be spread by the deer tick, caused by two bacteria called "the human granulocytic *Ehrlichia*" and "the human monocytic *Ehrlichia*," depending on which kind of human white blood cell the organism invades

ELISA test (enzyme-linked immunosorbent assay)—a technique used to detect antibodies in a person's blood or tissue sample

endemic—commonly occurring in an area

engorged—swollen, such as a tick's body after it finishes a meal of blood

erythema migrans (EM)—a migrating red rash, the first and most obvious sign of Lyme disease, more commonly known as the bull's-eye rash

host—an animal or plant that serves as a combination of home and food source for a parasite

hypostome—the tick's specialized mouthpart. It is long and slim and covered with barbs, like the barbs on a fish hook. The tick uses its mouth like a straw to suck up the host's blood.

immune—protected from a disease by antibodies that attack disease-causing bacteria

IV (intravenous) treatment—dripping a solution of antibiotic directly into the patient's blood through a tube attached to a hollow needle

juvenile rheumatoid arthritis (JRA)—arthritis that occurs in young children

larva—the second stage of a tick's life cycle, an immature six-legged tick that hatches from the egg

life cycle—the series of stages through which an animal passes as it develops into adult

lone-star tick—*Amblyomma americanum*, a tick found in the southern and southeastern United States that can spread Lyme disease

meningitis—an inflammation of the covering of the brain or spinal cord

molting—the shedding of an animal's outer covering during its development

nymph—the third stage of a tick's life cycle. This young tick is most active during the summer.

OspA (outer-surface protein A)—a protein on the surface of the Lyme disease spirochete that is targeted by Lyme disease vaccines

palps—"feelers," the sense organs that help a tick find a host

parasite—an animal that lives by feeding on a living animal or plant (its host)

PCR test—polymerase chain reaction, a technique used to detect Lyme disease bacteria

pesticide—a chemical that kills unwanted animals such as insects or ticks

spirochete—a spiral-shaped bacterium such as the one that causes Lyme disease

symptom—one of the effects of a disease

tick-borne disease—an illness spread by ticks

western black-legged tick—*Ixodes pacificus*, a tick found in the western United States that can spread Lyme disease

Western blot test—a technique used to detect antibodies in a person's blood or tissue sample

To Find Out More

Books

Landau, Elaine. *Lyme Disease*. New York: Franklin Watts, 1990.

Lang, Denise and Joseph Territo. *Coping with Lyme Disease: A Practical Guide to Dealing with Diagnosis and Treatment*. New York: Henry Holt and Company, 1997.

Murray, Polly. *The Widening Circle*. New York: St. Martin's Press, 1996.

Vanderhoof-Forschner, Karen. *Everything You Need to Know About Lyme Disease*. New York: John Wiley & Sons, 1997.

Veggeberg, Scott. *Lyme Disease*. Springfield, NJ: Enslow Publishers, 1998.

Organizations and Online Sites

American Lyme Disease Foundation, Inc.
Mill Pond Offices
293 Route 100
Somers, NY 10589
http://www.aldf.com
Information on Lyme disease and other tick-borne infections, deer ticks, frequently asked questions, and late-breaking news.

Don't Let Lyme Disease Interfere with Your Outdoor Fun
http://www.lymerix.com
This site features information about Lyme disease, the vaccine, and prevention tips from SmithKline Beecham, the maker of LYMErix™ vaccine against Lyme disease.

Evaluation of Three Commercial Tick-Removal Tools
http://www.biosci.ohio-state.edu/~acarolog/tickgone.htm
Researchers Richard L. Stewart Jr., Willy Burgdorfer, and Glen R. Needham report on a comparison of three tick-removal tools with medium-tipped tweezers for removing deer tick nymphs and adults.

Frequently Asked Questions about Lyme Disease
http://www.uhmc.sunysb.edu/lyme/faq.html
This site includes practical information from the State University of New York at Stony Brook

Lyme Disease

http://www.cdc.gov/ncidod/dvbid/lymeinfo.htm

Check out this site for up-to-date information and photos from the Centers for Disease Control and Prevention (CDC) National Center for Infectious Diseases, Division of Vector-Borne Infectious Diseases.

Lyme Disease

http://www.uri.edu/artsci/zool/ticklab/Lyme.html

This site, which is maintained by the "Rhode Island Tick Pickers," researchers at the University of Rhode Island, has extensive information on deer ticks, how Lyme disease spreads, and how to avoid the illness.

Lyme Disease Foundation

One Financial Plaza, 18th Floor

Hartford CT 06103

http://www.lyme.org/

This site features information about Lyme disease and preventing tick bites as well as photos of ticks.

Lyme Disease Patient's Guide

http://www.acponline.org/lyme/patient

At this site, you"ll find useful information from the American College of Physicians' Initiative on Lyme Disease: history, diagnosis, treatment, prevention, some common beliefs about Lyme disease (all false), and a glossary.

Lyme Disease: The Facts, The Challenge

http://www.niaid.nih.gov/publications/lyme/

This site is an online version of a pamphlet from the U.S. Department of Health and Human Services, Public Health Service, National Institutes of Health (NIH Publication No. 92-3193).

LymeNet Newsletter

http://newsletter.lymenet.org

Check out this e-mail newsletter published every 10 to 15 days. Back issues of the newsletter are also available.

Prevent Tick Bites: Prevent Lyme Disease

http://www.cdc.gov/niosh/nasd/docs2/as17000.html

At this site, you can read an article by Deborah Smith-Fiola of the Rutgers Cooperative Extension, Rutgers, the State University of New Jersey, September 1992.

Researchers Probing Basic Biology of Lyme Disease Bacterium

http://www.the-scientist.library.upenn.edu/yr1996/july/research_960708.html

This site consists of an article by Karen Hopkin from *The Scientist*, July 8, 1996.

Tick and Lyme Disease
http://familymedicine.miningco.com/msubticks.htm
This site features lots of links to photos of ticks and information about Lyme disease.

Ticks: Deer Tick (*Ixodes scapularis*)
http://www.ent.iastate.edu/imagegal/ticks/iscap/default.html
If you want to see lots of images of deer ticks (all four stages and both sexes) and movies of ticks crawling, check out this site from the Department of Entomology of Iowa State University.

A Note on Sources

Lyme disease is a topic we have been watching closely for a number of years. Our interest has been all too personal at times. We live in a New Jersey county that currently has the third highest rate of Lyme disease cases in the United States and, despite careful precautions, various family members have come down with it. Two family members have also participated as volunteer subjects in the testing of a new Lyme disease vaccine.

About 10 years ago, we wrote a book called *Lyme Disease: The Great Imitator*. In researching that book, we corresponded with nine Lyme disease researchers, who kindly answered our questions and suggested additions and changes for our manuscript. Dr. Leonard Sigal, Director of the Lyme Disease Center of the Robert Wood Johnson Medical School of the University of Medicine and Dentistry of New Jersey, was particularly helpful, giving generously of his time and energy to make sure we "got it right."

When it was time to revisit the subject for this book, we consulted available books and articles. We also obtained much helpful material from Lyme disease organizations. As with other subjects, we found that the Internet has become a rich and valuable source of information as well. A note of caution, though: Always consider the source of web pages. The information they contain is not always accurate or unbiased, and it may not be up to date. Chat rooms and newsgroups can be helpful, but they can also be dangerous. Remember that there is no way to know whether the people you talk to on the Internet are really who or what they say they are.

—Dr. Alvin Silverstein, Virginia Silverstein,
and Laura Silverstein Nunn

Index

Numbers in *italics* indicate illustrations.

Acorn connection, *25*
Adult tick, 28–29, *28*
Afzelius, Arvid, 13–14, 46
Amblyomma americanum,
    23–24
American dog tick, 29
Amoxicillin, 35
Antibiotics, 35–37, *35*
    making symptoms worse,
        36
    penicillin and EM rash, 14
    side effects, 36
Antibodies, 33–34, 41–42
Arachnids, 24
Arthritis, 21, 46
    and the EM rash, 14
    JRA, 9, 10
    Lyme arthritis, 10, 35

Babesiosis, 24
Bacterium, 12. *See also*
    Spirochetes

Black-legged tick, *22*, 23. *See
    also* Deer ticks
Books, 53
Borrelia burgdorferi, 13, *13*,
    18, 27, 47, 48
    old-time specimens, 14
    testing for, 33–34
    and tick larva, 27–28
    and vaccines, 41–43
Breathing problems, 21
Brinkley, Christie, 45
Buchwald, Alfred, 13, 46
Bujadoux, Charles, 46
Burgdorfer, Willy, 12, 47

Cats, 14, 21
Chickenpox viruses, 34, *34*
Clothing tips, *38*, 40
Concentration problems, 21

DbpA (decorinbinding pro-
    tein A), 42

Deer, 15, *15*
  and pesticides, 44–45
Deer ticks, 11, *11*, 15. *See also* Ticks
  and acorn crop, *25*
  and ehrlichiosis, 24
  percentage infected, 18–19
  and pesticides, 44
  size, 29
  where they are found, 23
Dermacentor variabilis, 29
Diagnosing Lyme disease, 31–35, *33, 34*
Dizziness, 21
Dog tick, 29
Dogs, *21*
Doxycycline, 35

Egg (tick), 27, 29
Ehrlichiosis, 24
ELISA test, 33–34
EM (erythema migrans) rash, 14, *14*, 19–20, 46, 47
  and diagnosis, 36
  when it appears, 20
Environment, changes in, 15, *15*
Enzyme-linked immunosorbent assay, 33–34

Erythema migrans. *See* EM

False results, 34, 35
Farming, 15
Fatigue, 9, 20, 37
Fever, symptom, 9, 20, *30*, 31

Garin, Charles, 46
Germs, 12–15, *13*
Gotz, H., 47
Guinea hens, 45, *45*

Headaches, 9, 21
Heart problems, 21, 35, 46
  and EM rash, 14
Hellerstrom, Sven, 47
Hiking, *16*, 40
Hosts, 24

IV (intravenous) treatment, 35–36, *35*
Ixodes dammini, 47
Ixodes pacificus, 23
Ixodes ricinus, 14, 46
Ixodes scapularis, 11, *11*, *22*, 23, 47

Joints, 9, *30*

JRA (juvenile rheumatoid arthritis), 9, 10

Laboratory tests, 33–35
Larva (tick), 27–28
Lipschutz, B., 46
Lizards, *43*
Lone-star tick, 23–24
Lyme, Connecticut, *6*, 7, 9, 10, 11
Lyme arthritis, 10, 35
Lyme disease
   background, 9–11, *10*, *11*
   cause of, 18–10
   complications, 21
   first observed, 13
   number of cases, 18
   timeline, 46–47
   who gets Lyme disease, 17
   why it spreads, 15, *15*, *16*
Lyme disease season, 28
Lymerix, 47

Malawista, Stephen E., 47
Meningitis, 14, 47
Mice. *See* White-footed mice
Migrating red rash, 14
Murray, Polly, 7, 8, 9, 47

Nervous system, 21, 35
Nymphs (tick), 28–29, *28*

Online sites, 54–57
Organizations, 54–57
OspA (outer-surface protein A), 41, 42
Outdoor hobbies, *16*

Parasites, 24
Parasitic wasps, 45
PCR test, 35
Penicillin, 14, 47
Pesticides, 40, 44–45
Pets, 17, *21*
Post-Lyme disease syndrome, 37, *37*
Preventing Lyme disease, 39–41, *44*, *45*
   clothing tips, *38*, 40
   removing a tick, 40
   vaccines, 41–43, *41*, *42*, *43*

Rash, 9, 10–11, *20*, 32–33
   EM rash, 14, *14*, 19–20
   migrating red rash, 14
Removing a tick, 40
Rocky Mountain spotted fever, 12, 24, 29

Sheep tick, 14
Shoes, what to wear, 40
Sleep disorders, 37, *37*
Sore throat, 20
Spiders, 24
Spielman, Andrew, 47
Spirochetes, 12–13, *13*, 20
   identifying the DNA, 35
Steere, Allen, 9–10, 11,
      12–13, 47
Stiff joints, 9
Stiff neck, 21
Summer, 8, 10
Swollen joints, 9, *30*
Symptoms, 8, 9, *20, 30,* 37
   recognizing, 19–20
   worsened by antibiotics,
      36

Ticks, *5,* 7–8, 11–12, *11, 20.*
      See also Deer ticks
   adult, 28–29, *28*
   American dog tick, 29
   description of, 25–26
   how long it lives, 27
   how they feed, 24, 26
   larva, 27–28
   legs, 24, *24,* 25
   life cycle, 27–29, *28*

mouth, 26–27, *26*
natural enemies, 45, *45*
number of legs, 24
nymphs, 28–29, *28*
removing a tick, 40
tick-borne diseases, 24
trapping ticks, *10*
what ticks eat, 8, 12
where they live, 18
which ones cause Lyme
   disease, 23–24
Timeline of Lyme disease,
   46–47
Treating Lyme disease,
   35–37, *35*

Vaccines, 41–43, *41, 42, 43,*
   47

Western black-legged tick,
   23
Western blot test, 33–34
Western fence lizards, *43*
White-footed mice, 28, 44,
   44
   and acorn crop, 25
   and Lyme disease, *19*
White-tailed deer, 15, *15*
Wood tick, 29

About the Authors

Dr. Alvin Silverstein is a Professor of Biology at the College of Staten Island of the City University of New York. Virginia Silverstein is a translator of Russian scientific literature. The Silversteins first worked together on a research project at the University of Pennsylvania. Since then, they have produced 6 children and more than 150 published books for young people.

Laura Silverstein Nunn, a graduate of Kean College, has been helping with her parents' books since her high school days. She is the coauthor of more than twenty books on diseases and health, science concepts, endangered species, and pets. Laura lives with her husband Matt and their young son Cory in a rural New Jersey town not far from her childhood home.